Cory
You are so
Smart and giving
Please do that
forever

Falling Apples

SELECTED POEMS

Endlesswill

Writer's Block Publishing
WWW.WRITERSBLOCKPUBLISHING.NET

Falling Apples – SELECTED POEMS

ISBN-13: 978-1092737616

Table of Contents

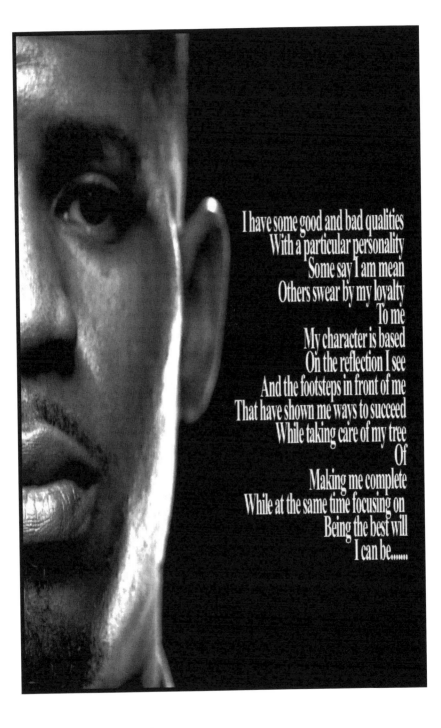

I have some good and bad qualities
With a particular personality
Some say I am mean
Others swear by my loyalty
To me
My character is based
On the reflection I see
And the footsteps in front of me
That have shown me ways to succeed
While taking care of my tree
Of
Making me complete
While at the same time focusing on
Being the best will
I can be.......

This book will allow you to understand me as an artist; with intention to encourage you to reach for your passion. We all have stresses that we deal with in life and just know that you are not alone in your struggle.

The title of this book "Falling Apples" is a connection to "the apple doesn't fall to from the tree" quote. As I am an apple, who has managed to roll away from my tree and plant new life.

This book is me, all of me, and all that I have to give; until more life is lived.

Introduction

Hello
My name is William Davis Jr.
And I am a product of a broken home
Underage drinking
Plus un-necessaries at my palm
I grew up in the hood
Main street being blunts lite
Cross street money get
Where sticks and stones could break your bones
And words would always hurt you
And when they do
Hold it in
Keep it real close
Then at the end of the day
Throw your feelings away
Because emotions
Don't mean anything in that world
Take my advice
Love life
And
When you fall
Smile
Then try again
But most importantly
Don't be afraid to fall twice
When you are vexed
Write
Share
And
Recite
But don't fight
As the world has shown
That the fight won't make it right

Falling Apples

Falling
A disconnect
Towards
Rotting
But not forgotten
Damaged fruit
Becomes food
For roots
Planting seeds
While the deeper
My apple is buried
Gives more chance for my seeds
To succeed

I know my falling
Isn't for me

Focus

You will miss out
On what is in front of you

Today

When your focus is still on
Yesterday

Arrogant

I've been called it all
Idiot
Dummy
Handsome
Smart
Stupid
I have even been called
A nothing
As if my being was invisible
Faded into the stereotypical of the norm
Being
Blended into the swarm
I have been called every name in the book
Of unassociated labels
And all of them
Every ill-advised title
Went through one ear
And through the other
Myself unable to comprehend
To those unwanted labels given
That judgment
Being a language that's foreign
But the ones that have
Held weight onto my shoulders
This dead lifting
Of names
Are cocky and arrogant
As if my confidence
To those that are quick to judge
Is scary to them
But what those labelers
Don't know
Is my story

How at 7
I witnessed my mother
Get thrown from a second story
Not a book
But a window
Now she has a scare on her forearm
From fragments
Of broken glass frame
This address of 7 inch stitch
To remind her of my father's
Way of dealing with pain
What my cocky
Doesn't reveal
Is my parents
Being ill
Sick with addiction
Drugs being
Conviction
What arrogance
Doesn't show is my parents
And the lack there of them being apparent
Like my preteen
Emancipation
Being grown at 14
Bills
Mixed with artistic
Skills
Homework
Flipping work
Bagged QP
The early introduction
Of weed
Instead of talks of birds and bees
Add that to a lack of Sleep
Multiply a 3.6 GPA
To the square root of 15+ points a game

Now subtract
No father
Or mother
There to shout hooray
At last seconds on the clock
Ball in my hand
And I hit that three pointer
To win the game
Whole team and stance calling
My name
The team winning
Doesn't
Equate to my missing
Or subtract
The terror of my mother's prison sentencing
Or add up to my father's hatred
Towards anything driven
How when he came around
It was always blunt hitting
Beer sipping
And talks
Of woman getting
This arrogant
Cocky
Doesn't
Reveal my scares
I have heard people call me cocky
But I call it
Triumph and overcome
And yes
I do see pride
Because I have cried
And I still cry
But on this page
I'm brave

Brave enough to spit poems
Of my sorrows
In front of strangers time and time again
Yet weak because I talk to my parents in segments
And see them rarely
And blame it on them living in Michigan
Yet I spend money on things
That can equate to a ticket
For a trip to visit
Most days
I don't like my parents
I have told them that I love them
In the same breath
That I have asked myself
What's wrong with them
So
I've accepted my burden
That my blessing
Is my question of their choices
This makes me accept my choice
To only pursue trying for new
While loving
You mom and dad
While being scared that
I'm an apples fall from the tree
To being just
Like you

Ghost

I died once
Maybe even more than once
But I really
Can only remember the last time
My thoughts and dreams
Being gagged by reality
Stabbed by unstable strides
Knife stuck in inconsistencies chest
Penetrating my last breath
Like a hole in the tire
Of a car racing on the road to success
But was detoured
To the cemetery of concrete expectations
I
Couldn't make it
My wants are now buried
Head stone reading
He wanted
So much more
So here I am
Just a ghost of that man that failed
Spirit living
To continue what my flesh only tried to do
It made attempts at purpose
But couldn't handle the burden of it not working
So it gave up
Jumped from tallest hope
Potential being rope
And choked
On foresight
Dreams dangling
Like the last leaf before winter
Absolutely having no chance of survival

But I tried
Tried
Is what I'm forced to remember
As if trying is good enough
But I know trying
Doesn't do a thing
Only reminds me of not winning
Recalls missing
And brings forth the memories
Of not being good enough
So I continue
As the ghost of misfortunes past
And a better man's future
Present state feeding on potential
Will I'm haunted by the hunger
Of what could've
Horrified by what didn't
So continuing
Is my commitment
This soul has purpose
Person was worthless
Unable to handle the hardships
So self-sank to the bottom
Of opportunities ocean
Drowned by the waters of what should have
And the deeper I sink
The pressure makes me think
That while I was alive
I was just weak
So this spirit
Takes the place for what will be
A better man
Now stronger
And with these new ghostly powers
Walls don't even make sense
I just walk through them

Continuing to move forward
Nothing can stop me now
I laugh at blockades challenge
Because ghost don't worry
They just don't
I now have the ability to make others
Uneasy
With just me being
While others don't believe what
They witness
As they are forced to remember
That for one to die and survive
Is just a lie
But that doubt only feeds my stride
Powers my prize
Of conquering this life
With a driven existence
Day by day
I am just a ghost
But those woes
Are my lows
That have made me into
This ghost
Dead to doubt
But funny thing is

That I'm better this way

Note to Self

I can only be creative
My melanin surface is my soil
My entirety is Earth
There is so much more
Implanted within this Will
Thoughts watered with will
Driven
Foot
Full force to the pedal
As I pick the poems from the rose
Of concrete growth
Chanting
Success loves me
Success loves me not
Success loves me
Success loves me not
A game of Russian roulette
Played with foresight of dreams
Not yet met
So I plant plans
Proceeding to break ground
A seed to life
And I
Can see the light
Born blind
But by my stride
Has given me foresight
So again I grow
Weather comes
But I grow
And think about it
A plant survives off of the sunlight
And it also lives through the night

That next day
When you see it
It's different
It's stronger
More vibrant
It doesn't worry
So why worry
Is that rhetorical question
That's repeated
So I can remember
That my roots have spread
Strengthening thought
Making room for growth
And when flower sees the sun
When I see the sun
And my being
Puts connection to source
Plays math
With their laughs
And embrace each day
Equaling a positive
It does something to me
This feeling you can't really name
As if newborn
Crying to light of first sight
And when it feels its mother touch
When baby presses life to heart
It stops crying
Life is calm now
When I write
It's my calm down

Wish

A wish
Is only amazing
To those who want
But
For those that dream
A wish
Is just another
Task for them
To achieve

Hurt

I'm hurt
Hurt like
A simple conversation like
"I'll be back"
Turning into a 7 year long return
Walking back through the door
A missing
Of too long
And getting used to it
From seen at 13
To again at 20
A missing of mother moments
Being more than just moments
I'm hurt like
I'm used to it
Disappointment coming as often
As penny thrown moments in a fountain
I wished things were better
And it's funny making wishes
When you know deep down in your soul
That wishing won't make anything happen
I'm hurt like
A piece of me believing that a wish
Would change things
More hurt that
That piece in me
Is gone
That vulnerability with blind innocents of focus
The tunnel vision of potential distractions
That
World at your fingertips look in your eyes
For me has been gone
Because

As my past experiences
Have shown to circle around
Unfavorable
It just seems so unrealistic to hope
When you learn early that
Santa
Easter bunnies
And tooth-fairies
Are a joke
With laughter only being apparent
To mask anger
Then you get used it
Like
I remember the first time
I ever drove
Father comes home drunk
High
Hurt
Or
God knows what
And me
Been waiting there for 3 days
For him to pick me up
I'm 15
Angry
And not a least bit worried of where he had been
Because this wasn't
His first time vacationing at my disposal
But this time
I had to get home
As my home
Was not his home
I lived about 2 hours away
A drive on main streets
Highways
And

Now accompanied by inexperience
I lived with my friends
As case in point
By story being told
My parents where to good at abandonment
So for me
Rely on
Was about as loyal
As my father's acceptance of responsibility
And this day
His consistency
Wouldn't evade him
As he reminded me
In order for me
To get home
I would have to drive
It is now 11:30 pm
On a school night of a Tuesday
After
Just missing Monday
A 2 hour
First time ever drive
To escape him
I looked at him
Felt nervous
And thought

Why not

New

Sometimes I have to sit in silence
Really shut out all life's noises
To let my mind vent
As I think of where the time has went
I try to make an attempt
To focus on my choices
Choices made
And those to come
Comparing the man I wanted to be
To this man that I have become
While contrasting on the difference in the two
As I question
Have I changed from being me
Or
Have I just evolved from the person I used to be
And now I am this

New

So as I look back
I reflect
Yet
I have a hard time trying to accept
This into of what I grew
This makes me wonder
If I am really ready for a

New

Life

Direction

Praying for direction and the ability
To control this aggression
So as I write
I treat this as my confession
My words helping me to express
Because as sad as it may sound
My poems know me the best
So I see that as I write
My mind is reflecting what it sees
To map out the directions
That I need to be complete
To fully be me
Which would mean to succeed
And finally knowing that my mind is at ease
So I ask
When will I have it
Happiness being a habit
My mood on average
While accepting not questioning my blessings
Or is that impossible
A mere concept that's illogical
Something only found in stories
Is true happiness never having a worry
And living without a fear
Or is it knowing that trouble will come
But a solution to the right direction
Is always near
Then I question the mirror
If my reflection is right
Have I left my problems in my rear

Which direction do I go

Bitter

I'm bitter
Been broken down
Head low
Like the self esteem
Of unfilled dreams
This missing on a foresight for supposed to
While my person repeats to itself
You are a winner
Bitter
For always needing to win
Angry that there is even a game to play for the win
Sometimes the game played
Being amount of
Cash you get
Title you represent
Or
Number of relationships
Maybe even a game of
Shirts and skins
Colors and flags
Kneel and who's standing
Nationality
Gender
Or religion
Or job
Or street
Or gang
Or education
Or finances
So many more
Or's
I'm bitter
Because of our Or's

Our needed
Self-convictions
These restrictions
On our minds
As if our thoughts our boxed
Chained
And locked
To what we are taught
Imagination evaded
For "needed" education
Of hatred
Comparison
And
Not being better than
I
Am
Bitter
Broken
And beaten
Most days
I feel defeated
As my legs move in motion of routine
Life's treadmill under my feet
Awake
Work
Sleep
Awake
Work
Sleep
Repeat
Repeat
Repeat
I'm bitter
Because
I am starting to notice it

As I'm trying to focus on
Commit
Eyes targeted
Again
I'm focused
Like
Predator onto prey
Food being opportunity
As the chase mirrors my accuracy
While disadvantage
Makes me miss
But I don't quit
Those things the world sees of me as
Another stereotype
Good but just not quite
One out of every number
Potential
Prison number
Fallen number
Another trying to be more
Than just a number
Which makes me a number
Just
Bitter
But I'm just glad
That I'm starting to notice it

Adversity

As I wake up and look in the mirror
The first thing I see is adversity
As I am aware
That today
And every day following
This world
Will attempt to bring out the worst in me
Conflict and restrict
My since of urgency
It will look
At my will
My drive and motivation to better
Me
Will
And make a slight slit into my wrist
Blood will drip from my finger tips
As I watch the red unload
Myself daily dying slow
My wrist resembling me
And the blood being my goals
While the world holds the blade
This daunting reality
Being my daily approach
Surviving in times
Where the world seems so cold
Being burned
By the heat of night
While my days are left froze
Falling into the grasp of self-compliancy
Begging myself
To keep fighting the world

So I go

Yell

As we are yelling
I think are souls are lost
Wandering towards right
While our bodies are distracted
From the displacement of the masses
The lies of eyes attractions
As we are accepting being the constant subject
Of ours societies subtraction
With ever pistol pop
But we only know what we are taught
So we fight
Shout
And
Judge
Forgetting
Love
Trust
And
Us
Leaving us
Lost

So we yell-out everything that comes to mind
Instead of begging and pleading
For what is needed to find
Our

HELP

<u>Missing</u>

I'm missing good yesterdays
As I anticipate my
Tomorrow
In a day filled with
Sorrow
Yesterday's memories get
Borrowed
While passion prepares me
For a bettering tomorrow
I've accepted the embraced challenges now
So good days intentions are
Followed

Tear to the Eye

One day
A lonely TEAR
Dripped past a dry EYE
And TEAR asked EYE
Why don't you cry
The EYE replied angrily
With red passion of hurt
Fueling its words
Why should I
I've done that before
And it only leads to more cry
This path of let down
Head down
And
The wishing for different
This gazing for better days
And the wanting to be pure
So EYE asked TEAR
Why cry
What purpose
Would be given
From unwanted liquid
Cries only represent
The giving in
And not being able to handle what's given
As the EYE continues to rant
The TEAR listens
Glistens
And shimmers from knowing
Of its worth
TEAR pays attention to EYES words
As the EYE finishes
The TEAR embraces the EYE

For replenishment
And then reminds EYE
Those emotions can never be hidden
While TEAR holds the EYE
The TEAR reminds
And makes the EYE remember
That the shedding
Is the forgetting
And making of new
TEAR looks at EYE
And says
I am here for you
So let go of the pain that you hold
And let me
Hold you
As they embrace
TEAR falls from EYES face
And EYE no longer can escape the feeling
Of washed away
This cleansing of a new day
As EYES pains slowly fades away
He begins to thank TEAR
For helping erase fear
TEAR smiles
Drips down
Begins to fade
But before it leaves
To vacate to its next needed place
The TEAR says
I am always here for you
But most importantly
Thanks

End

All good things
Come to an end
But for the great
Not even death
Can be an escape

Death

Why do we disrespect

DEATH

Our living suppressed
Cancer being relevant
Yet people still smoke cigarettes

DEATH

Living through lies
Constant complacency in our eyes
Our faults and struggles
Will lead to our own demise
This eventually will lead to
More

DEATH

When I Die

When I die
Will there be hundreds of people at my funeral
Or was my character
And
Personality only good enough to impact a few
I have done some good
And less bad
I've told lies
But mostly told the truth
And if you add my intensions
Plus good with expenses
Subtract anger and a lust for riches
Would it equal proof
Sometimes I think on the left side
What's the use
And
Then the right side says
That's just an excuse
Look ahead at life and live bigger than regret
And live life for its laughter
Never stressing of death
But am I just repressing the stress
Laughing on the outside
But actually feeling upset
Everyday more quick to flip

But is it only a test

Thanks to those

Because of you
I am me
I can be
Me
My unique
My free
Because of your tears
I am here
Without fear
Just free
To see
What I can be
Because of you
And your pain
Your chains have been my gain
As I think about your scars
I promise myself that they will not be in vain
For every time you were forced to bleed
Each blood drop
Drives me to succeed
For every meal you didn't eat
Gives me strength not be weak
For every moment you endured
Reassures me that I can handle more
So as I live my life
I
Want
For
Yours

Content Capitalism

Can I talk to this country's conscience
Content
The constant violence and the abundance of death
As if there is an unbeknownst body count contest
A much needed conversation
On the separation of races
Our acceptance of segregation
And the willing but unwanted reliance for wealth
Or let's just talk about being mis-educated
Our knowledge being provided by the nation
Whose ulterior motives
Is their power being in control
And the reminder of us as a people
Staying in our strings' attached role
By enforcing its fear
The ultimate puppeteer just demanding its rules
Of move when told move
And prisons and stories
Told by rebel corpses force us to just believe
In this imperfect system that's teaching us follow
While destruction takes lead
It's sad how our vision seems to be so incomplete
We are all perfect leaves burdened by broken trees
Dreams being our shedding but our un-forgetting
Allows advance to blow in the breeze
Under these laws of corruption
Nothing is changing
Just more clouds of gunshots
And the raining of bomb drops
And the re-programming of our brain
So many questions without answers
As we wait for a better
When will we realize that we are the change

And we use words like hope to replace our efforts
Oh Miss America
The mother of our nation
We are breastfed your broken bread of hatred
While our imagination
Invents these complacent creations
And the glorification of nothing
You
Life giver of lies
And the appreciation of bluffing
Oh Miss America
I hate this picture that you repeat
Canvas being bloodshed on an easel of deceit
Paint brushes of mislead
Painters' passion filled with greed
Oh Miss America
Why do you enjoy
Watching your land bleed

Limbo

Where does that put you
If you're standing between
Past bad decisions
And
Future good intentions

Officer Davis

She tells me
No
She demands that I to call her
Officer Davis
She tells me
And has told me for the last 2 and 1/2 years
That she wants to be a police officer
And when I ask her why
Her reply is
"The world needs saving"
And she is very aware that the super hero's
The Batman's
The Wonder Woman's
And the speed of light flight of
The man in blue tights
Are not real
So
She says
She will be a real hero
That she is going to protect people
And I'm scared
Because I know
My daughter will
Her will is that of me
Multiplied by 103
My daughter at the age of 9
Is so brave
And strong
Out of all my kids
She is the one
I rarely see cry
She always goes to her room
Every time she is upset and hurt

I asked her why once
And she told me
With her head held high
That she leaves
Because when she is sad
When she is hurt and angry
That
That is her time
Her strength is amazing
I remember one time
My son's
Almost got into a fight
Not sure over what
But before I could even speak up
She
My daughter
Asked them
Why
Before they could even give her a reply
She reminded them that they loved each other
And to play nice
They listened
Without
Any friction
They just listened
My daughter
She is a leader
I'm so happy to have her
Honestly
I need her
So I'm scared
Of her passion
Her need for protecting
Because the relevance of the disrespecting
And, "hate the police," statements
How they are viewed as the one profession

That is the poster child for hatred
And the trending videos
Of them beating
Tazing
And sending
Innocent lives to the grave
I'm not sure how
My daughter
Little miss officer Davis
Is going to fit into
That system

America

In real life
Gay means happy
Faggot means
A bundle of sticks bound together as fuel
Nigger means ignorant
And bigot means America
Where we can redefine words for belittlement
Place judgement upon opposition
Any opposing opinion that's different
Looks different
Smells different
Walks different
In America
We don't like different

Oh beautiful these raciest skies
And make up covered pain
America
America
God shed his grace
We are in need

Where our mascot
Is a gun shot
Being released
From the palm of the wicked
I mean innocent
Because the one holding deadly weapon
In hand
Seems to be the medias victim
In this taken
I mean
Given land

WE ARE PROUD
We show pride over our colors
These proud flag decorative colors
Red
Meaning blood sweat and tears
White
Right
In the middle of bold bountiful
Star filled amazing
Above the blue
This place of beauty relevant to blind bitter
Showing dis-appreciation to our forgotten
America
WE ARE PRIDE
So proud we look forward
Ignoring blatant
Un-blanketed cold
A world fully unclothed
This bare all nakedness of nothing
A braggadocios exposing of what we got
Step wrong
Get shot
Wrong place
Get robbed
And broken hearts are the tools for malpractice
Because the abundance of abused come
10 a dozen
With tax included
Visit now
And we will even throw in a lifetime subscription
Of worldly opinion
At the one-time payment fee of personal space
Our face is this book titled
Fast food
Rude

Research medication induced
Depression
Contents
Aggression
To hide our eyes wandering
On our surroundings
From our 15 sec attention spans
We are so
Lonely
With over 15,000 friends
And a penny short of a million followers
But yet
No cup of sugar to borrow
While this world is so large
We preview its beautiful view
And we get our news
With our head low
America
Where the
"WHY DO IT TODAY"
"WHEN YOU CAN DO IT TOMORROW"
Trumps
The work ethic
That was set
From the leaders we have shown
So much disrespect
And we only miss on days
That are calendar has set
America
We are preprogrammed
Told when to work
How to work
How to eat
What to eat
When to celebrate
Who to celebrate

Who to hate
Told who to date
Who to think is in first place
And after this commercial break
We will get back to our regularly scheduled
Program of the day
A real life version of first 48
Where our life is on the line
And the officer
Doesn't care who did the crime
Just as long as we get life
Come on in
Any and all are welcome
That can handle our requirements
Just remember
Don't be you
Don't break anything
And follow our rules
Even if they seem
A bit against you
Just remember the most important
American
Thing
Enjoy yourself

Animals

If reincarnation is something
I can't wait to be
Not human
Symbol of divide
Contest
Compete
Greed
This ugly unstable constant
And the repeat of the same day
I want to be a lion
Or maybe a bird
Or even an elephant
Anything but this
I really
Really want to be more
Because us
Humans
We haven't figured it out yet
That
We haven't figured it out yet
And
It seems like we will never figure it out
Religion
Gender
Race
Finances
We seem to need
To be complete
While every other species
Just
Lives
Like sometimes
I wonder if

Bluebirds hate canaries
And if
Red robins hate crows
Do eagles hate hawks
Or
Do they just look up to the sky
And fly
Looking down at our life
Using wings to soar over our
Separation
Our
Segregation
Do they feel sorry
For our hatred
And wonder why
Or do they just fly
While we
Die
I watched one of those
YouTube
Documentaries once
And it explained
That a lion
The king of the jungle
One of most
Respected
And feared animals
Will only eat when it's hungry
Meaning gazelle
And lion lives in harmony
Drinking from lake together
Living together
Existing
Together
Gazelle knowing of its fate

Of eventually being ate
But it lives until then
With that being said
Maybe
Hate is just hungry
And obviously
Diversity
Is its favorite munchie
I find it so
Funny
That we can call
An animal
Savage
Wild
So we cage it
Hunt it
And name it
And if
Its
An animal
That is really wanted
We kill it
And frame it
Then we have a person
Who society
Deems as worthless
Savage and wild
So we cage them
Hunt them
And
Name them
And if it's a person
That is really wanted
The world kills them
And media gives reason to frame them
Deeming person as worthless

This helps us to blame them
Most days I question
And I find it
So
Embarrassing
That we can't even comprehend
The comparison
Of how equal
The way the world treats an animal
To the way
We our
Treating
Our
Own
People

Apologetic

I'm sure when we ALL die
That the first thing God will do is apologize
God will say
Sorry for the many shades
And the hues of our different views
This
Lack of understanding of what he/she created
I'm pretty sure God
Will say sorry
Confident that he/she will explain color
And let us know that we took it all out of context
Then God will ask
Why were we so scared of color
Why were we so proud of color
He/she will ask,
Why did we put so much importance on beauty.
He/she will explain
To the point that
Imagination implants
Imagery into explanation
And God
With such conviction
Will tell us simply
That on one rainy heaven day
He/she was feeling creative
So God began a beautiful painting
And we
Our colors
Was what was created
Letting us know that every unique color used
Made perfection
And from his/her point of view
When he/she

Our God
Looked at that creation
He/she
Didn't see hatred
Discrimination
Or pride of importance
on different portions of his/her painting
He/she just saw God
Which is us
Meaning you
I'm sure that God will then wave hand
Create a massive rainbow
With the beauty of a newborn
Innocent soothing
And
God will ask us
Which one of these colors
Represents your worlds hate
With no answer to speak
God will then teach
That every one color
Every shade
Every hue
That we view
Is God
Meaning you
And
He/she will then say
I am so sorry for all the confusion
God will then tell us
That it doesn't even matter now
Because we are in heaven
God will then laugh
Mocking our coined phrase
Of

God don't make no mistakes
And again he/she will apologize
For the black
The white
The yellow
The red
All these colors
And mainly the un-comfortability
Of what our eyes seen
And what we decided to worldly point out
And God will explain
That we are now one
We have risen above the clouds
So smile
Put outer down
Lay to bury the worry and pride of our outside
And God will then open arms wide
Consoling away our much needed lost
With a hug
And he/she
Our God
Will let us know
That we can
Finally live now

Write it

When the words are too heavy for the poem
So you don't write it
Pen sheds tear because it can't right it
So you wait
Allow mental
To lift the weights of worry
Want for better
And more worry
So you get into position
Flat back
Knees bent
Feet pressed onto the floor
Holding down doubt and you push
Struggle
Yet you push
Struggle
Yet you push
Repetition representing
The routine of these streets
Struggle
Yet you push
Struggle yet
We push
In need of an uplift
The strengthening of our gifts
While the struggle is the reminder of your choice
That no one is making you do this
Yet this "this"
Is what no one else will do
So when the words are too heavy for the poem
You must allow the poetry to
Write you

One Day

One day
It will all just be O.K.
But today
The skies are gray
I'm sitting silent in the rain
Waiting for sun rays
Right now
It's clouds and the weather is wild
Earthquakes everywhere
And thunderous sounds
Lightening hitting the ground
And it's dark all around
But somehow I still manage to smile
In the heart of the storm
I can calm its growl
As I'm needing the sun
Just a glimpse of its rays
Yes I'm yearning for the sun
These dark days
I need to be done
Sun shining and green grass
I'm begging to come
And I know it will be better
With the break of bad weather
So today
I will pray
That tomorrow
Will be O.K.

Want and a Need

I find it difficult to distinguish the difference
Between a want and a need
I've considered relating a want to greed
Because you may have all you need
But you still long to exceed
And you do everything to earn it
Often going through extremes
It seems a need is similar to the air that we breathe
Because you couldn't survive without it
Even though it seems to be the littlest thing
Like can you imagine a bird
Without the ability to sing
Or a brain that lacks the capability
To think of the simplest dream
It's obscene the uncanny difference
Between a want and a need
But without one there wouldn't be the other
Like niceness to mean
You just need to know how to prioritize the two
In the correct categorize
And that statement is relative
Because what you consider a need
May be different for me
And a certain want for you
Probably would be silly to me
But serious to you
And it's crazy because most of the time
What you want
Is seldom what you need to do
So my wants are my needs
That's how I'll distinguish the two

Success

We are taught to
Trust
Obey
And
Believe
What we are told
What we read
And what we see
As our mirrors are distracted
By this distorted
Platform of world beauty
While our reflections cry out
For us to believe in what you see
But as we focused on our dreams
Society reminds us
That it is unnecessary
To want more than what's been given
While there isn't much left to get
So my question is
What is really success?

Peace

Yesterday
Is gone
While today
Lives on
But the joining piece
Between the two
Is the peace the days
Can be for you
So live

Reason to Smile

What if you could hold onto the reason you smile
Would you question it
Or just realize
That's the true meaning of what a blessing is
To just literally be happy and accept it
Even if the situation is exceptionate
You accept
100 % happy
Joyful
Ravishment
Anger not being relevant
Life filled with embellishment
Or is that even possible
A concept that is illogical
For me
While still considering life's constant obstacles
I still jump and enjoy my everyday
While still at the same time knowing
That it is up to me
To find ways for anger to avoid me
Because I believe that anger destroys the
Feeling for serenity
So I smile each day while building a better me
Laughing and not letting my downs distract me
Or allowing the attitudes of others to attack me
Inner peace
Where my soul is on the beach relaxing
My present is a track meet
And my past I have lapped seeing
The future as that flag
While all at the same time being glad
Knowing my smile is genuine
Not a mask

Us

I told her that
I don't believe in love
She looked me in my eyes
Smiled
And confidentiality said
I don't believe in love
Either
I just believe in us

Too Much

I have come to the conclusion
Placed notary stamp on realization
Literally just stop wondering why
And have accepted
That I think about you way to much
For some strange reason
You come to mind for no reason
Like
When I wake up to take my head off of the pillow
And thank God for the ability to do so
Something in me
Also has me thank him for you
And I smile
Which makes me think of your smile
And now I'm happy
Not even 5 minutes into my day
While taking the time to pray
Mixed with recalling images of your face
And I'm happy
Ready to concur the world
Fighting with hope in hand
And anticipation as my shield
Prepared to defend my joy
That's what you've done to me
All from just a kiss
A moment that replays in my mind
Of a time when my lips were stained from your
Perfection
I can still taste your smile
It reminds me of an ocean breeze
Mixed with the warmth of the sun
And a hint of strawberries
Those are all my are favorites

And when I kissed you
Those are the things I were able to taste
So relaxation is what your flavor is
I really do think about you too much
But if me thinking
Is my way of seeing you more
Then I'm sure that I'm not thinking
About you enough

<u>Goodbye</u>

I
Want
To
Be
Your
Favorite
Hello
And
Your
Hardest
Goodbye

No Wife

I don't want a wife
I don't want warm meals
As I walk through the door
Or laundry folded placed in my dresser drawer
And I definitely don't want your appreciation
Don't thank me
Praise me
Or even think of me
I don't want a wife
I just want you
I want you at your enjoyment without me in mind
Don't consider my feelings
Please just be
I want you
To be
Comfortable
I've heard that the person you are
When no one is watching
Is the person
That you will inevitably turn out to be
So please pretend I am blind
As my eyes are covered to any and all
Besides
The touch that you are willing to gift
Don't think too much
About messing up
And with your permission
I'll even help you fix it
I want to be in your trust
Can you love me like your favorite things
I ask this
Because
Everyone knows that favorites don't change

I want to be that always picked
Those jeans that are ripped
Worn out a bit
And may have a few un-washable stains
But it is something about them
The memories they bring
I don't want to be a husband
That replaceable worldly burden
I want to earn your forever
I don't want you to have the pressure
Or suggested prioritize of a wife
Can I fit in your life
Like those jeans that hug you just right
I want to be like your favorites
Place me on your minds mantle
Of keep sakes
Right next to your favorite place
Of where you would vacate
Because when you're with me
Your thoughts should be at ease
Sit back and enjoy loves breeze
Feet up
Comfortable
Without a care in the world
I don't want to be a husband
And
I don't want a wife
I just want us to know
That we are
Forever
Welcome in
Each other's life

Bee

I'm sure God laughs at the
Irony
How my allergy is a bee
This busy beautiful
Needed in the world
And one sting directed
Aimed
And hit
At me
Can be my worse
Then on the reverse
We have this busy
Needed in the world
This
Beautiful being
An all completion of me
Whose sting has been
The best for me
This being
Being my Cathey
I'm sure God
Laughs at the
Irony

Cathey

I find it hard to compare
This much relaxing
As if I'm laid back flat
My face adjacent to the stars
On a 84 degree summer night
Flavor
Taste of a breeze
With a hint of peace of mind
An evening of perfection in the form of weather
My gentle
Catch of feather
Some would describe this as the perfect day
I call this moment
Cathey
Also known as a daydream
And I have nicknamed her
Comfort
Comfort like soothing hand on a long walk
Backdrop ocean
Sent of sea salt
Mixed with the gift
Of good emotions
I am lucky enough to be in love with amazing
A real life super woman
Her powers are to embrace
Focus
And at lighting speed pace
Chase after her wants
She appears to the world as a smile
An uplifting growl
Strong enough to teach the world
Confident like mother lion
Hunting down food for her young

She is
Fierce and strong
Strong enough to take care of a pride
You see Cathey
But I often call her
Pride
Because I am proud
Honestly
I can't help but to tell her
I love you
I look her in her eyes and I confess
My heart thumping
As if lungs have deflated air from my chest
I am in aww
Star struck
By this celebrity
My body stiffens
And I begin to get nervous
Like school boy
Blowing kisses at his crush
On the playground
Seconds after spinning on mary-go-round
She makes me light headed
Each time I witness her beauty
She is peace
I call her my life
And I promise to love her
I have heard people call her Cathey
And I am fortunate enough to call her
Wife
And I have nicknamed her
My forever
And forever
I will love her

I love you
Cathey

Mona Lisa

My Mona Lisa
In my art gallery of Polaroid pictures
She stands out
This image is taken care of
Hung delicately on my mantle
Loosing these others photos would hurt
But being without my Mona Lisa
That is something I couldn't handle
I treasure this portrait
Other images are blemishes
But this is just gorgeous
Others minimal
My Mona Lisa enormous
A prize
Just to have this image on my eyes
To stare into those eyes
Is a gift
Something to me that is just so priceless
She is my unique
My magnifique
My everything
She has everything I need
My admiration feens
And feels absolutely amazing
Knowing she is here for me
She is mine
My art
My perfection
My Mona Lisa

<u>Trying</u>

I cried today
Let me be honest with you
I cry most days
Most times when you leave in the morning
Seconds after you kiss my face
And tell me to have a good day
But never before
You walk out the door
I'm too prideful to ever let you see my tears pour
I'm scared
Scared of you not being there
Scared of me not being there
And more so scared of the day
We don't want to be here
I hope that never comes
But considering where I'm from
Born to the norm of fight
Can't get right and hide
I'm numb
Broken emotions plus this unfixed figure
I'm aware that that equation lacks patience
And seems to only embrace escape
I only ask that you continue to have faith
Because honestly I love you
And I feel like I'm close to actually knowing
What that means
As I emulate the way you look at me
But if doing for you as you do for me
Is the only thing my loves brings
I'm scared that I have yet
To fully understand what
Loving you means

Face

Today be the world's ugly
Unafraid of your natural
I want to see you at your most comfortable
I know you have been tricked into thinking red lips
Makeup
And all the other cosmetic stuff
Is what's needed
But believe me
That fresh face off the pillow
Followed by that yawn
Which tells the world hello
That moment
That look in your face
Squinted eye
Bare all and un-shy
Hold it
That is your beautiful
When you accept
The need for no approval
Unbothered by standards
Grown
So no need to be pampered
With
Blush
Primed hair all done up
To eventually be taken down
And rinsed in a drain
To the graveyard of fake self esteem
Where each tombstone reads
More beautiful then what the world's eyes
Could ever see
I promise you
You are perfect

And I don't mean perfect to my standards
Because my validation
Is like telling grandma
That the food that she made tastes good
She already knows it
And kind of scoffs at any approval
I ask that
Just as she is confident
In her cooking
That is how you should feel
About the way that you are looking
You are beautiful
Like ocean waves
Being blessed with the light of sun rays
Perfection
Like rainbow arisen after rainy day
Each color in its place
Ladies
Please
Love and admire
Your face

Daughters

Entertained by my daughters clapping
Four palms
Below messy
Ponytails
Fluttering
Beautifully like rainbows
Filled with the color of butterfly wings
Their fingers
Painted at the tip
The hands of perfection
More amazing then a thousand poetic snaps
In a room of filled with
Pens perfected
Make words from a poem
Feel like
A king on his throne
These sentences being seated
Next to
My princesses

Favorites

Think of your three favorite things
Any three things

(Write them down)

1._____

2._____

3._____

Stop

Hold those favorite thoughts
Thinking of that times they made you smile
Remember why you picked them
Now next time you get down
Remember your three
Think of the feelings they bring
Then
Try to cheer up

Lake

Today be a lake
Constant
Needed
And calm
Today live like a lake
As a pebble of worry breaks your surface
Let your under not be distracted
As for deep down
You know of your worth

Dear Students

Dear Students
Today
I asked you to listen
As it was my intention to teach
But
The constant class distractions
The unnecessary question asking
The backpack fumbling
The under the breath mumbling
And the paper crumbling
Just all of the
EXTRA
Made it hard for me
To give my educational lecture
And you students question
My frustration
As I've explained
And explained
Rephrased
And explained
But yet you say you don't get it
I blame it on your effort and the lack thereof
Plus your opposition of commitment
Then you wonder why you get the grades you get
Dear Students
I have to say it again as I am sure
You have stopped paying attention
Me acknowledging you directly every so often
Is required
Is what I have learned
Class repeat what you just heard
What's this word
Stop playing

What did you say
Young men keep your hands to yourself
No you can't go to the bathroom
Class please get quite
Students focus
I said students focus
Why must we digress
Dear Students
I want you to know
That my heart I am giving you
Myself once falling victim to a distraction
So I am begging you
Pleading and
Asking
That you
See you
As I
See you
Which is this person of strength
Don't appreciate my effort
And don't give thanks
Just respect that I know
That you all have what it takes
You all are amazing
You just have to embrace it
Class is about to be over
So let's go over
Today's lesson
You all are amazing
When you try
And effort should never die
Tomorrow's homework
Which everyone should have
Is to write a letter to
Your future you
Think of all the things you would ask

I think that went well
Tomorrow
They will turn in their homework
All of them
I am sure of it
I can't wait until tomorrow
Because today they understood
Good morning class
Please get out your homework from yesterday
What
You don't have it
What do you mean
You don't have it
Raise your hands if you have it
Higher let me see your elbows over your heads
Reach for the success
That I am trying to show you how to achieve
And realize that it is in arms reach
A stretch for a better next
Which seems obvious you don't want
As I try to teach
Reach
And educate
But you would rather procrastinate
Or even worse evade
So it seems
That reach for you students
Is a self-sabotaged missing
Leaving your want for accomplished dreams
Empty
Dear Students
I hope one day soon
You all will wake up

Tomorrow

I can't wait until my tomorrow
Because as I live today
Going about my way
Not really knowing the right things to do or say
I think about sorrow
And things I should have done
Places I should have gone
But didn't
A mere victim of my today
My present
My neglect
My self-disrespect
Of wrong choices
So I think about tomorrow and ways to avoid this
Disappointment in me
And positions I have put myself in the past
To face defeat
Avoiding succeed
I want to insure that it isn't on repeat
So I can ultimately achieve
Knowing that I failed
And learn from it
To insure the mistakes don't happen twice
To encounter the same situation
But being able to handle it right

To be right

So as I awake and go about my day
I wait for the night
This is then followed by my promises
Of tomorrow

A Letter to my Eyes

Dear eyes
I would like to start off by saying
I don't believe you two anymore
At the young age of 30
I realize that you both lie
You've deceived me into believing
That what I seen
What
You see is what I get
But that
That is not true
Mere illusions
Just tricks of deception
And I wonder
Question why
Why would you do this
Have me chasing
Like a dog
Wanting a play toy
No
Many play toys
Thinking I would
Or
Could win what you
My pupils
Had me chasing
Running full speed
Heart racing
Anticipating a prize
Racing on what I thought was life's track
But was really a treadmill
Going nowhere fast
After a goal

That you seen
Made my mind believe was truth
But was really a mirage
My brained drained by fantasy
Again I don't
Won't
Believe you anymore
And I ask you both
Eyes why
I question
Why choose deception
I remember the first time they begged
For that Thundercat action figure
"Thundercats hoooo"
I loved that cartoon
My sister said it was doll
But I wanted
They
My eyes made me want it
Fully tricked out action figure
With pull back Snapping arm
Detachable sword
I already had the pajamas
I had to have it
My eyes convinced my brain
That I had to have it
On television
My vision thought it could fly
And my eyes were so mesmerized
That my mind
Was blind to reality
Knew of the lie
But I
They
My eyes
Made me want it

So I begged and pleaded
Eyes made me feel as if I needed it
Then I had it
It didn't fly
The pull-back was weak
The thing lasted a week
I was only 5
Now 25 years later
You still lie
How dumb of me to finally see
That what you see
Is not real
Only fabrication
That fuels aggravation
So you both
I promise you
You only there for appearance
Don't cry
You have done this to yourself
Making me
Mislead
Me
I will no longer follow your lead
I'm sorry
I feel bad
That you both
Are just
Sorry

With much regret,

Endlesswill

Reason

What is your reason
I'm asking
What is your reason
For eating
For getting
And not just needing
For trying to succeed
For simply trying
When those times
Come to
Remind
That you need a reason

What is your reason?

Who are you

Are you a person out for wealth
Are you one out for self
How would you describe yourself
Are you selfish
Are you helpless
Are you lost
Or more close to being found
Are you a person that people enjoy to be around
Can you look at yourself in the mirror
And truly be proud
Are you sad
Are you mad
Are you glad
And if you are one of any
Can you answer the reason why
Do you cry
Are you shy
Are to consumed with pride
Are you afraid to die
Or are you afraid of life that
While you live you just lie
Lie to yourself
Lie to others
Lie in the bed underlying in covers
Are you a brother
A lover
Who are you
What are you
Where should you be
Can you see
Deep inside
Truly open your eyes
To the person that you truly are

Or
Do you choose just to hide
While being scared
So unaware
At the potential in you
And the person that is really there
If
Who are you
Was the only question on a questionnaire
What answer would you put there
So again I ask you
Who are you

Will

I realized a long time ago
My soul is focused on free
Compared
Apples to oranges
Or
Grind to hold back
That I'm just a different breed
I see the world's attentiveness
To being a victim of societies
Indifference
Its struggles are dwelling upon
Eyes engagement on repeat
While I walk
No I run through the heat
Knowing
Either way its go hurt
So
I might as well get through it wanting
With willingness depicted as self sufficient
My minds twisted into never giving up
Always going
Fall go
Stop no
Just go
See my grandfather's
Name was Will
My fathers
Name is Will
And you see
I am
Will
Rolling through this passing of names
A tri

Cycle
Of try
In pursuit to do
And you see
I'm the last Will
Predecessors have stopped and
Popped
From the rolling on roads of owns obstacles
But I go
Determination fueling my
Never flat
Passion as petals
And I move
Legs pushing
Constant as ocean waters
Swaying with waves of dreams saved
From those nights
Where anxiety has kept me awake
I'm dreaming
Arms reaching to be seated on a pedestal
Of my preparedness
You see I have been scared
And the only thing I learned from that
Is that you anticipate to runaway
So I've learned
To be brave
Face to face to dismay
With doubt at my back
While the black that is my fact
Is unfortunately a societal set back
But like I said before
I run through the heat
Pushing will
Up hill
Climb is my only fate
Focused set on great

Because honestly
My world is way bigger then me
Behind me
Stands
Lays
Eats
Plays
Learns
And
Follows
Behind me my family
Follows
So how could I not be seen
Myself being the scene of
Samuel chapter 1 verse 17
Goliath: Life
David: overcome
And me: that rock
A weapon of small testament
The winning is moving forward
Hitting surface of
SHOULD NOT BE ABLE TO WIN
And breaking past expectations
Instead of simply making connection
And
Just settling
I've named myself
Endless
My father gave me
Will
Webster's dictionary defining
Aforementioned word meaning:

"To have a wish or desire"

So I've accepted that I'm a life of pennies
Being passed in a well
Wishing silently for want
While desire allows penny thrown moment
To calm the constant of never complacent
A break from chasing worldly appreciation
Racing against stereotypes
Towards my right for personal greatness
As I embrace this gift to write
While my palm unwraps
My present
From the trap
Of the world's eyes
Of another falling of track
My view
Is
Has been
And
Will forever
Be
Will

Memory

As I give you this art
That you read
I must admit to you something
And
Please be hesitant to start judging
But I
Am scared of
ME
Horrified of my possibilities
Because I know of what I have done
Thinking I am pursuing right
But setting myself up subconsciously to do wrong
So in reality is wrong what I really want
Or more so what I really wanted
I feel haunted
By a ghost of this man's memories
And tormented by the skeletons in his closet
Unfortunately that closet is mine
As I lay awake at night
Afraid of the lies rising up from the dead
Freeing themselves from the prison in head
And making themselves present in my present
Feeling threatened by my reflection
And the secrets he may tell
As he laughs when we are eye to eye
And I am left to just yell
Because despite that I stand with pride
There are things that I still hide
And even though it may seem
That I have succeeded
Deep down I feel that I have failed
Internally defeated
Covered with the stench of

Dead dying dreams
As the fumes forever follow me
As a reminder
A remembrance
Of the times of my lack of commitment
Like
Sinning but yelling Christian
At one time
Being married and falling victim
To not playing my part
And being deceitful
Using these words as a flute
Charming snakes
Right out of there baskets
Then
Simply attacking their hearts
Using them simply as show pieces
Trophies on my mantle
Committing suicide without knowing it
Trying to pick apart relationships
When in the end my heart gets dismantled
Self-heart surgery
Ruining my wants
Literally standing in my own way
Running with shoes untied
Knowingly blocking the pursuit of my purpose
At times I have felt so worthless
Like I'm eyes closed searching
For something
Then when I feel as if I have found that something
I open my eyes and see nothing
All hopes let down
Living through the tears of a clown
Because even though you see me smile
Deep down
I may have already drowned

From the tears that I didn't
Or couldn't let out
Internally flooded
From my attempts at victory
But fallen slightly short
Treated life as a game
Often hating to play
While being a fan of the sport
My own contradiction
My conscience feeling conflicted
Because I've fallen victim
To dwelling on negative times
So my rights are restricted
Thoughts are twisted
Intertwined thinking torn between
What I have seen
And what I want to see
As I try my best to not let my yesterday
Truly define me
While preparing my present
For a positive future
So my bad memories
I treat as mementos
Reminding me to grasp more
That's how I reflect
Or more so
Respect my past thoughts
How do you
Retract on yours

Unwanted Repeat

As my thoughts battle with the silence
I pay attention
While anticipating wants that are
Halloweened as needs
And the foolery of false focus
While accepting that
Studying for success
Doesn't make for dealing with failure
With a straight face any easier
It only makes the optimism of trying
Dry
Worn out and abused
As if the token played
Should have been saved
And
The game was a fake
Deception
Trickled with the taste of trickeries
A ploy
Only to be won by the selection of the chosen
How dumb of me to forget
Those victories are won by entitlement
And living the life of hands open
To receive trophies by those that deem worthy
SUCCESS IS GIVEN
That vision
That mission statement of how to make it
You know the one that is constantly mistaken
The
Hard work pays off
Statement
FORGET IT
As a matter of fact
Place that sentence in the section
Of your intelligence where fairytale stories rest

You know those lies
That the world has unapologetically
Made you deal with
Like the fabrication of Santa
Or the idea that you will ever order a burger
And it will look like the commercial
They call that false advertisement
But I call that my father
Because I have accepted that it could be better
But considering lack of effort
That I will always be forced to just accept
And pretend to be OK with it
These moments are called magic
Entertainment for the mind
While embracing for the embarrassment
Of the situation that you have been placed in
A race won by shot of the gun
Repeated
But forever living with coming up short
By unwanted circumstances
And resources not accessible
To the rest
Only purposed for that one
While I'm forced to be comfortable with
Being better than
But apparently less of
So vengeance is masked behind a smile
Considering not being dealt an even hand
And companionship of course management
And chosen trophy-men's partnership
Lead to their upper hand
Some would label this routine
As a lopsided victory
I call this my everyday

Failure

Failure
Is and only is
A life without
Doing

Talking to the Old Me

How can you be angry
Because you see that I have changed
When you haven't seen me since 2005
And I don't even look the same
You need to update that photo
In that picture frame in your brain
Because my personality has made an upgrade
And the past me was just a childish phase
My introductory paragraph
Why are you still stuck on that page
I consider it growing
While your focused on the change
And you look at it as being weak
But realistically it's me being brave
Because I realize that I have my kids to raise
And again while your focused on the change
I'm focused on building a business
So my kids can be paid
Giving them security so my kids can be safe
So yes
Maybe I have changed
Because when I was 16 living care free
Back then I didn't have kids to save
So yes
I appreciate you acknowledging
The difference I am
However
For you to be so surprised
You should be ashamed
That just brings forth the thought
Of your lack thereof effort to do the same
Which would seem your conscious is on concrete
Stuck

Pasted
A brain that is wasted
Eating food without tasting it
And it's sad
Because if you were to take a chance to be aware
You would be amazed at the potential growth Tha
t's there
And don't try to relate to me
Because the person I used to be
Is the only one fair to be compared
To the growth that I've staired
Meaning I've carefully prepared each step
Enhancing my intellect
By looking at my yesterday
And doing today what I haven't done yet
While thinking of tomorrows plans
That I will put into effect
Realizing that my change reflects
These words that I speak from the left of my chest
Poems pushing my growth
To help change the affect
Of that repetition of regret
So I am only subject to success
So yes I agree
I have changed
And I question why you haven't done the same
It seems like your reality is a repetition
And for you to show anger towards me
Because of it
Leaves me no other choice but to feel conflicted
As I wonder at the reason for your resentment
When in fact
You are the reason
Of your own restrictions

Growth and Change

Growth and change
Two concepts that are one in the same
Because can you truly grow
Without the mindset of changing
Or can you really grow while still maintaining
Without erasing or changing
Somethings in your mind frame
But wouldn't that alter your attitude
Towards thoughts to develop
Because without changing to grow
The same things in life will not help you to get up
By changing we're growing to appreciate
The things that are not with us
So take a chance
And by growing
You're allowing yourself to enhance
Take a risk
Fail
Learn from it
Then do it again
Make sure that your mistakes aren't on repeat
Take your time and prepare
So the next time you'll succeed

Sacrifices

I make sacrifices in my life
To give my kids
The best
I guess if you don't think I'm right
You can get
Left

Attention Poets

Attention poets
And those who enjoy poetry
You are now in tune to the worlds
Example of a fool
Because I can't follow rules
Educated more than the traditional school
Hard knocks being my hallways
Doubt being the everyday and growing up
To bare minimum wage pay
Is what I seen for the anticipation for better days
But luckily
I woke up
My eyes taking flight to insight
Seeing in me so much
While talents
Are my talons
Under an eagles wings
I woke up this morning
Arose
Petals being pen to paper
Stem broken a little at the end
To mimic the system
That tries to keep us broken within
While we are forced
To unfortunately enjoy it's sent
You see
I've been sent
To put sense into negligence
And wake you up to your truth
Because honestly
I am such a big fan of you
As my words play street curb
To the routine of these roads

I'm giving you a comforting hand to hold
So I ask
Can you walk with me
Let's stroll past the old
And learn something new
Don't assume that me speaking is preaching
No
I'm not here to praise
I'm here to raise expectations
As for generations of frustration
Leads to the complacency of separation
In this weak maze
We call
Sunday through Monday
So if one day
(might even be today)
You have a burden to share
Place that weight on me
I promise you
I'll listen
I'll unload that heavy
That you hold
So you can be free and feel the breeze
Of flying
Inside
Living in ease
My only request
Is that release all of that heavy
On your chest
You must confess
All of that congest
Allow simile to sooth
Yes
Be angry
Upset
Channel energy

And then let your pen move
To that healing of a poem
Palm
Calms
And
Creates this
Canvas of a conversation
A spoken master piece
That helps push past your reach
As poetry shared
Is a path for peace
So I welcome you
And I'll put focus onto
The painting that you drew
My attention statuted
Glued
Into the trying to understand
The feelings you are going through
As emotions are expressed
Through written depiction
But most importantly poet
I'll listen to you lift
The weight of worry
Off your chest
So
Attention poets and those who enjoy poetry
Step up to the stage
Allow emotions to be brave
Share wants transferred from a page
And put transgressions to rest
So audience
I look forward to whose
Next

Used to

"Super Nintendo
Sega Genesis
When I was dead broke
Man I couldn't picture this"
-Biggie

Now that was Hip Hop
I listen to this
New music
And I can't help but think
Please just stop
Put those bars behind bars
And those
Simple preteen
16's
Still got a lot of learning to do
Enroll them in hip hop summer school
Where *Nas* is super intendent
And *it was written*
That
Jay Z teaches history
And outlines *the Blueprint*
To the heart of the city
DMX is the gym teacher
Explaining that to push up in this industry
You must get off your *belly*
Rakim facilitates science
As he explains how to be a *God MC*
Amongst giants
And
Biggie walks you through
The *commandments* with math
And to pass
You must be spittin'

Either freestyling
Or something that's written
And if you mumble
You're suspended
Like
Hip hop
I know I grew up with you
But the older I get
I realize that I just can't
Mess with you
The way you enjoy what these lames say
With those minimal lyrics
Mumble rap word play
And the
Bruh....
Admit it though
That beat do bang doe
No
That just sounds stupid
That's like eating Ramon noodles
On a diamond plate
Or enjoying a stomach ache
From food you just ate
Because
At the end of the day
The results are still the same
When you sit and digest
And allow your body to rest
It still stank
Sometimes I wonder
If music is art
And rap is music
But everyone is a rapper
Are there any real artists
Or maybe I just can't understand the context

My conscience a little too complex
For lyrics that really lack content
Compressed with a bunch of rhyming words
About selling birds
Smoking herb
Woman with curves
Manly self, self, self
Hip hop is meant to have a message
Not lusting for wealth
The true purpose is to help
Not hate
Which is remanence of hell
Or selling yourself for records to sell
It is art
Which is supposed to evoke feeling
I remember the first album
I literally couldn't stop listening to
It was Jay Z's Black Album
Track number 7
Threats
Was my morning motivation
The metaphors
The clarity in his cadence
The imagination
It was perfect
And just last week
I downloaded
XXL's 2017
New hip hop artist mixtape
And to say the least
That was a big mistake
It was worthless
My ears where mad that they even heard it
Like I got a headache from the intro
And couldn't make it past
Track 2

And I realized that instead of the
Molly's
Lean
And
Percocet's
Hip hop
We need you to put some poetry
Back in you
Please bring it back to that fire
So to all artists listening
I ask that you take a chance to inspire
And
Not make music that is looked down upon
But
Art that is
Admired

Confidence

My confidence is a consequence
Of my life's journey so far
You see I'm aware I'm not close to the finish
But I know I've walked really far
As you can see from my scars
I have walked one foot in front of the other
Pushing past the constant talk
Ignoring the whispers of others
Just focused
While being positive that every step brings me
So much closer to approach this equanimity
This peace
So I pace myself
And phase out the potential problems
Every step that I take with pride
Always walking looking forward
With my head held high
This helps strengthen every stride
Walking because I'm too tired to run
Just tired from being tired of simply being tired
But I can't stop
Mindset that my next step is my goal
And with my determination driving my desires
My focus is set on go
As I wake up and look in the mirror at myself
That image reminds me of the struggles
That I have closed
Appreciating the concrete from which I rose
Considering the lack of care, constant life's wares,
And each battle to get the adequate amount of air
I've still grown

Critique

So you want to critique my speech
Warning
A lion doesn't lose sleep
Over the opinion of a sheep
And only makes me think
If I write like you
What's the use of being me
My style may not be right for you
But this attire was inspired
From something a lot higher
Than your opinion trying to suppress me
I laugh as your negativity
Aims directly at my personality
Personally your input
Needs to be put into
A bag thrown in a trash
Or maybe even recycled
Turned into something useful
Like a paper for me to write on
So then your view would be right on
So thank you
For being a pessimist
But I bet my last dollar
That you more than likely missed
The depth of dreams
Written down
As my art
My passion
This abyss
So
Unwanted opinion
Don't judge my pen

Forgot

I would tell you that I still think of you
But that implies that one day
My thoughts for you had stopped
And to be honest
You're a moment that cannot be forgot
Complied around so much
Everything
Memories of the beginning
Almost loves first steps
As we held hands
Balancing one another to walk upright
However the pressure we placed
On one another's shoulders became heavy
And what we thought where feelings
Were apparently weights
Masked in a loving wrapping paper
Each day we were excited to open
Just portions of our supposed gift
Unprepared of the Pandora's Box
As we dug deeper into each other's souls
Revealing secrets and scars that weren't closed
Our past overwhelmed our pursuit
We attempted to plant seeds
Even watered a few
But our garden wasn't in the right light
So it's not surprising that we grew apart
Both played a part
In mixing together the ingredients
Of anger
Bewilderment
Push and pull
And sprinkles of love
To make the elixir of lust

A poison
Being sipped by trust
Loyalty being drunk
Distorted by shots
Taken without hesitation
Failure driven
Knowing that it's illegal to drive under intoxication
And we were well over the legal limit
So how could we make it home
When we knowingly forced our crash

Conflict

How can I begin to comprehend
This simple conflict in our relationship
This lack of trust is the pirate on satins ship
Driven through fire
We both are liars
So ashamed
Who's to blame
Can it change
When hearts are hurt
Can it work
When feelings are ignored
You call me a dog and I call you a whore
This pain is heart surgery
How long can we endure
You yell and say that I am no longer yours
Because you can't fight the sight of
Another woman caressing my pores
Which is followed by you crying and
Slamming the door
As I beat on wall while pictures fall on the floor
Glass is shattered
Thoughts are scattered
And so are feelings
Is there a healing
Some say yes
But we both question if we are able to accept
The weight of us choosing neglect
Along with the depth of regret
So this is it
The lack there of commitment
Will be our deficit
All our love irrelevant
And anger will now take precedence

Broken over mistakes
Love just thrown away
Because it's so much easier to escape
Than to look at each other's face
So we chose to run away
Avoiding confronting the chooses we made
While questioning
If we are only cheating ourselves
By simply skipping to the next page
When the story was getting so good
But instead of fighting it out
We leave because we could
And most said we should
Then there are times when you wish that would
Have tried again
Remembering great times in the relationship
But then reality sets in
That putting our conflicts over our compassions
Is what really made us end

Goodbye

Smiles

**Smiles
Tell
Lies
Words
Can't
Express**

How

How am I to survive
In this generation
With all of this hate and frustration
Better yet
How do I take care of life
With this constant devastation
When I am so persistent
To the point it's been called pushy
How do I teach patience
And get my children to comprehend
That all good things come to an end
So the reach
Is only worth reaching
When you are reaching
For the greatness within

Canvas

How are we supposed to change the image
When the canvas is already painted
Before we even admire the beauty
We lust before we dated
And know this gift we have to offer one another
Has now been tainted
But again
That's just the canvas that is painted
Painted by society
In so many different varieties
Growing up we see so such infidelity
That blind eyes can see
Television shows with single parents
Endless stories of failed marriages
So many that
Who would even know where to start
I'm just saying that it seems inevitable that we all
Have broken or have had a broken heart
So truly can we view that relationship canvas
As a work of art or just a picture that is viewed
Past along and used
Thrown to the back and abused
And is only looked at when we get that
Urge of loneliness
Then tossed away when that canvas
Gets annoying to us
Because everybody knows
We can always get another picture
But isn't it crazy how those
Mona Lisa's
Picasso's
And Van Goh's
Stick with us

Branded into our memory banks
There so we can appreciate
A well taken care of canvas
And simply glance at the fake
But now-a -days even forgery is desired
As the effort of duplication is admired
And still hung in a frame
But my question is, if that masterpiece isn't real
Isn't it just a game
An art gallery of facades
Pretends or merely fakes
And considering this worlds view on relationship
I question if we as artist can originally paint
Look at that tarnished
Broken and neglected canvas
And see something great
Calmly using precise brush strokes because
This should be your escape
Your getaway from the restraints
But we only know what we are taught
So eventually our time and efforts go to waste
We look at that canvas we created
And throw it away
Because the colors are not as vibrant
But believe me I have seen amazing shades of gray
So I refuse to never not paint
I will portray that perception
Of more than just affection
And hold on to my canvas until it is
Wanted not neglected
Treasured and protected
So I've got a priceless painting for sale
And I'm looking for an art gallery
Do you have any suggestions

Change

Fortunately I have realized
That my style of speech
And way that I think is unique
To the person that the world sees
As perception is reality
And past problems
And viewed image
Show my posters image as a
- Fit description
- As pull over
- Put hands up
- Young man sit down
- Shut up and score touchdown
- or un-justice, unsolved, and he might have deserved it victim

This constant told direction
Or question
Which makes me question
Why am I being questioned
Then in turn leaves me confused
Perplexed and vexed
By our history of abuse
Like I get it
Skin tone
Different languages
Different clothes
Different Hair
Really
Anything that's there
I am starting to understand
World press for distain at something
Or anything
It doesn't understand

Like no
I don't agree
But I get it
It wants me to get
And never forget it
Hatred is like riding a bike
The moment you learn
You'll never be without transportation
As history shows
Hatred will take you places
It's encrypted
Everywhere
Sports
Posters
Almost all television
This distasteful craving for hate
Like
I can remember
Watching hate at an early age
Most mornings before school
Bugs bunny cartoons
Elmer Fudd so quick to shoot
Or Garfield and Ottie
With Garfield being so rude
An unrealized programming of getting used to
But now
I try my best to change my mindset
In this world
Where we are filled with hate and repress
So I question

How do I change?

Today

Today
Love
And
Learn
Unconditionally
Don't apologize for life
Or
For death
Today
Just
Live
And
Love
Life

Hillsborough

With Occoneechee beneath my feet
I am towering above my worries
The scent of BBQ
Wrapped
Amongst the flow of the Eno River
My soul reminds me
That this is my home
A town fit for a poet
So much so
That there is a street called
Poets Walk
Where present writers
Can hear the whispers of remembered stanzas
Footsteps on the pavement
Resemble the page flips
Of past poetry books
And the concrete overlay of sealed cadences
Accompany all that are on that stroll
I have told myself
This place
Of Hillsborough
Is where I will write my story
A story with illustrations painted with the feathers
Of a "Purple Crow"
Pages packed with neighboring art galleries
And a Truffle or two or three
I have been welcomed with open arms
As my arms embrace you all with poetry
Limbs being my pen
And I embody this calligraphy
I'll write
Recite
And share

And more importantly care for your appreciation
Of this literary art
My destination
Is the unity of a community
With poetry being my spark
Because I have learned and want to help teach
That passion is a protection
When times are dark
So you see a poet
A father
A laureate
You read a poem
But I am giving you
This town
My home of Hillsborough
My heart

Christmas

My Christmas smells like morning smiles
As wonderful as new life
Being breathed for first time
Opening eyes to blessings
Where kitchen plates of pancakes
Are interrupted by fingertips opening gifts
In anticipation
For a long awaited remembered want
My Christmas is sweetest dreams
Wrapped in a cloud filled with hugs from my kids
Forever raining love and growth
A holiday season with the meaning
Of missing family that you see with
Imagery that is so apparent
Even when you just speak on the phone
As they describe decorations
And much awaited presentations
While giving
Eating
And us sharing stories
Like
You remember that one time when Granny won
The lottery and bought everybody mountain bikes
Some of us
Mainly me
Still learning how to ride a bike
But the good thing is I learned
I grew
I knew that she bought me that bike bigger
Because next year a gift might not be there
So I grew
Since then a little younger than ten
Christmas to means

Growth
Anticipation to gift bigger
A present of positive passion holding hands open
Vulnerable
While accepting present blessings
I want to shower this world with gifts
Cloud bearing will
Raining down drive
Of being an un-traditionalist
I don't fight the good fight
Each day awoke is a present
And to me living life is the gift
With wit and my heart open
With a pencil grip
My Christmas
Is this togetherness
Santa being lived in rooms of smiles
While each individual bears gifts of willingness
Our Christmas list being this moment
As we hold it
While letting go of it
My Christmas is a giving
While thanking you for receiving
I appreciate this
I waited for it
Last night I was a kid again
Up in anticipation with joy in my spirit
Sleep deprived
While Christmas day is what keeps me awake
As poetry and comradery are my December 25th
Again thank you
For being a
While giving
And accepting present gifts
Thank you

Blind Artist

What if a blind person drew Jesus
How would they illustrate his facial features
Would the artist even draw a he
Maybe the configuration of the pencil and paper
Would create a she
I often wonder of the image
More so maybe a blemish
Because supposedly
Jesus died
Was brought forth in front of eyes
So can the true magnitude of that miracle
Be recreated
Or
Merely mimicked with imagination
Can one actually paint greatness
To me
Every time I see a picture of Jesus
I can't help but to think of time wasted
With the many configurations
Blue eyes and white hands
Or
Brown skin with hair like lamb
So many variations of just one
I'm curious of how God feels
About the image we have of his son
Or if we are to worried about a portrait
Resulting in the halting of blessings to come
Instead of just appreciating the son
I find it scary that the image
More so it seems then even the message
Is what we place the weight on so heavy
Making the picture
An unneeded necessary

How to make it

Directions on how to make it in America

Lesson 1:
Don't be different
Don't be black
And if you are black
Don't take offense
Of being reminded of it on a daily basis
Those that make remarks
They aren't racist
They are simply comedians
Practicing there comedy on the first
Oppressed person
They are comfortable with
Noted oppressed person don't get angry
As the self-entitled
Entertainer of the moment
Doesn't know any better
The entertainer's actions
Are typically inherited and learned behavior
So
Unfortunately correcting the behavior
Won't do anything but confess the situation
So
Don't knock them out
Passive aggression seems to work best
In this situation
Subtle eye rolls
A quick attack at entitled entertainers
Starbucks intake
Or love for pumpkin spice
Has always been acknowledged attacks

Lesson 2:
Don't be white and dress black
(whatever that means)
Warning if you do
You will be mocked by others that are white
Laughed at by those that are black
So
Do not confuse stylish gear as clothing
No
Each race has a uniform
So white people
No more Jordan's
We all know he only wants the poverty
Stricken folks fighting
For that well put together
Made in China
Proud to be an American
Jump man
Note
If you are white
Your uniform from now on out
Is only business attire
Professional
Well-earned and respected
2 parent
Privileged household
Tighten with a tie
Sealed of approval
Lesson 3:
Don't be Muslim
Warning
Don't be Muslim
You all are the worst
The reason for aids
Slaves

Hunger
High gas prices
This whole beard epidemic
That hipsters find so trendy
Terrorism
Jordan's being so expensive
And of course
We all know that Muslims
Are the reason Winter is so cold
Muslims if that is your life choice
Don't do that here
In this land of the free
Home of the enslaved to the media
And what they portray
Again don't be black
Don't be white and act black
And don't dare to be Muslim
Don't date outside your race
Matter a fact
Get a mirror
Look at it
Call yourself ugly
Unwanted
Make fun of your passions
Then pretend to love yourself
After you are ashamed of the hurtful
Things you have spoke
When you feel like your life is a joke
Then only then will you be a successful
Less confident
Incompetent American
And you will proudly probably get a job
Or even can run for president
Welcome to America

Stranger

In
A
World
Full
Of
Neighbors
What
Is
A
Stranger

Can't Sleep

When the pen
Won't let you sleep
So you ink
Poems think of meaningful moments
That has been placed before the
A night of write
Clouds hovering over passions rights
While the moon light
Shows paths
To paper lines
Wind blowing
Whispering
"Is everything alright"
As the only answer
Is the connection of felt tip
And open notebook scent
So you release
Accepting you will sleep
Only when the poem is
Complete

Black Out Poetry

-A blackout poem is created when an artist takes a marker
(usually a black marker) to an already established text and
starts redacting words until a new poem is formed.

Introduction

always

end

importantly

Direction

My best

write
reflecting

my

possible

happiness

so

I go

When I Die

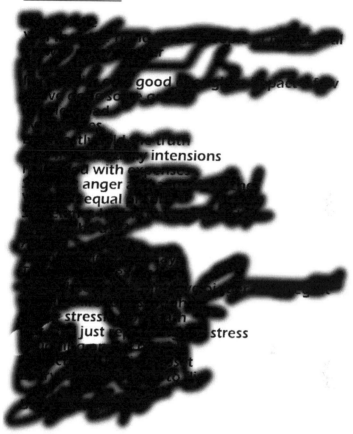

good

intensions
with
anger
equal

stress
just   stress

Thanks to those

Because 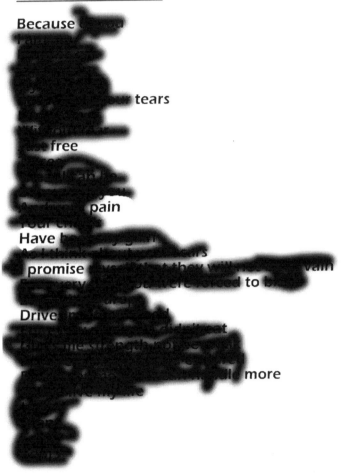 tears

free

pain

Have

promise

Drive

more

Write it

When ██ words █████████████████████
█████████████████
██████████████████████████
██████ wait

██████████████ worry
Want f██████er
And ████ worry
█████████████████

█████████████████████████
██ █████████████████ push

█████ push
█████████████████
██████████████
████████
██ █████
██ ███ █████
██████████████ our
█████████████████████████████
█████████████████
████████████████
████████ e words ████████████████
███████████ the ████████
████████

Want and a Need

Reason to Smile

could

happy

Even

enjoy

me

not

my

smile

Trying

Most

tears

hide

honest

love

CREATE YOUR OWN
BLACKOUT POETRY

Tomorrow

I can't wait until my tomorrow
Because as I live today
Going about my way
Not really knowing the right things to do or say
I think about sorrow
And things I should have done
Places I should have gone
But didn't
A mere victim of my today
My present
My neglect
My self-disrespect
Of wrong choices
So I think about tomorrow and ways to avoid this
Disappointment in me
And positions I have put myself in the past
To face defeat
Avoiding succeed
I want to insure that it isn't on repeat
So I can ultimately achieve
A willing
Able to fail and learn from it
To insure the mistakes don't happen twice
To encounter the same situation
But being able to handle it right
To be right
So as I awake and go about my day
I wait for the night
Which is then followed by my promises
Of tomorrow

Growth and Change

Growth and change
Two concepts that are one in the same
Because can you truly grow
Without the mindset of changing
Or can you really grow while still maintaining
Without erasing or changing
Somethings in your mind frame
But wouldn't that alter your attitude
Towards thoughts to develop
Because without changing to grow
The same things in life will not help you to get up
By changing we're growing to appreciate
The things that are not with us
So take a chance
And by growing
You're allowing yourself to enhance
Take a risk
Fail
Learn from it
Then do it again
Make sure that your mistakes aren't on repeat
Take your time and prepare
So the next time you'll succeed

Critique

So you want to critique my speech
Warning
A lion doesn't lose sleep
Over the opinion of a sheep
And makes me think
If I write like you
What's the use of being me
My style may not be right for you
But this attire was inspired
From something a lot higher
Than your opinion trying to suppress me
I laugh as your negativity
Aims directly at my personality
Personally your input
Needs to be put into
A bag thrown in a trash
Or maybe even recycled
Turned into something useful
Like a paper for me to write on
So then your view would be right on
So thank you
For being a pessimist
But I bet my last dollar
That you more than likely missed
The depth of dreams
Written down
As my art
My passion
This abyss
Unwanted opinion
Don't judge my pen

Blind Artist

What if a blind person drew Jesus
How would they illustrate his facial features
Would the artist even draw a he
Maybe the configuration of the pencil and paper
Would create a she
I often wonder of the image
More so maybe a blemish
Because Jesus died
Was brought forth in front of eyes
So can the true magnitude of that miracle
Be recreated
Or
Merely mimicked with imagination
Can one actually paint greatness
To me
Every time I see a picture of Jesus
I can't help but to think of time wasted
With the many configurations
Blue eyes and white hands
Or
Brown skin with hair like lamb
So many variations of just one
I'm curious of how God feels
About the image we have of his son
Or if we are to worried about a portrait
Resulting in the halting of blessings to come
Instead of just appreciating the son
I find it scary that the image
More so it seems then even the message
Is what we place the weight on so heavy
Making the picture
An unneeded necessary

THIS BOOK IS A DEDICATION
TO POETRY, FAMILY, FRIENDS, AND WILL.
WILLIAM "ENDLESSWILL" DAVIS CONTRIBUTES THE
UPMOST GRATITUDE AND APPRECIATION TO ALL HIS
CONTACTS FOR LISTENING, CRITIQUING, AND
BELIEVING IN HIS TALENTS.
WITHOUT YOU I WOULD HAVE NEVER
PURSUED MY PASSION

-THANK YOU ALL-

WILLIAM "ENDLESSWILL" DAVIS JR
2017-2018
POET LAUREATE OF HILLSBOROUGH, NC

SPECIAL THANKS TO

JOSIAH, JANIAH, JAIDEN, JORDAN, AND MADI, WITHOUT YOU ALL;
I COULDN'T IMAGINE WHERE MY LIFE WOULD BE

CATHEY, MY WIFE, THANK YOU FOR YOUR EVERYTHING!

IF YOU'RE INSPIRED WRITE YOUR OWN
POEMS, NOTES, RESPONSES, SHORT STORIES,
DRAWINGS, MATH PROBLEMS, JOKES,
ANYTHING JUST #WRITEHEAVY

Notes: